The WONDER of It All

Copyright© 2001 New Leaf Press / Master Books, Green Forest, Arkansas

Concept, design and production by Left Coast Design, Portland, Oregon.

ISBN: 0-89221-493-7 ⊱ Library of Congress: 99-69243 ⊱ Printed in the United States of America. ⊱ 3rd Printing

All photography by **Steve Terrill** unless otherwise indicated. Cover (repeated page 14), **Panoramic Images**; page 1, **Digital Stock**, (*Four Seasons*); page 13, **Index Stock**; Page 18, **National Geographic**; page 19, **Digital Stock** (*Four Seasons*); page 24, **Masterfile**; page 26, 27, **Digital Stock**, (*Storm Chaser*); page 34, 35, **Digital Stock**, (*Stormchaser*); page 40, **Digital Stock**, (*Animals in Action*); page 44, **Ibid**; page 45, **Digital Stock**, (*Animals in Action*); page 47, zebras, **Digital Stock** (*Animals in Action*); page 50, **Superstock**; page 52, tornado, **Digital Stock** (*Storm Chaser*); page 55, **National Geographic**; page 56, **Digital Stock** (*Animals in Action*); page 58, upper left, lower left, **Digital Stock** (*Animals in Action*); page 59, **Digital Stock** (*Animals in Action*); page 60, left, **Digital Stock** (*Nature and Landscapes*); page 61, **Digital Stock** (*Animals in Action*); page 66, 67, **Tony Stone Images**; Page 68, 69, **Digital Stock** (*Nature and Landscapes*); page 71, **Digital Stock** (*Nature and Landscapes*)

Please visit our website for other great titles: *www.newleafpress.net*

The WONDER of It All

THE CREATION ACCOUNT ACCORDING TO THE BOOK OF JOB

The Book of Job [is] what this writer, at least, believes is the most fascinating book in the Bible. The climax of its message, though unexpected, is intensely practical, with special relevance to the needs of God's people in these days of widespread humanism and evolutionary scientism.

Skeptics and liberals often deny that Job ever lived. To them, the story of Job is pious fiction—a great dramatic poem no doubt, but no more historical than other ancient epics. This contradicts the acceptance of Job as a true record of events by both the ancient Jews and early Christians. The author of Job presents his narrative as a true account, and it would have been blasphemous for him to describe events taking place in heaven and to devote four chapters to a verbatim transcription of God's words if it were merely a vehicle for him to present his own philosophy.

Many expositors maintain that the main theme in Job is the mystery of suffering. Job himself had no solution [to the problem of suffering] and desperately appealed to God to provide one while steadfastly maintaining his faith in God and in an ultimate resolution. So, then, what is God's solution? When he finally enters the dialogue himself, what does He say about this vexing problem of human suffering? Amazingly, God says nothing about it! What He does talk about is creation . . .

This leads us to the remarkable conclusion that a correct and complete doctrine of creation is the answer to all the problems that burden this present hurting world.

The four-chapter message direct from God that climaxes the Book of Job is unparalleled by anything else in the Bible. Even unbelieving scholars acknowledge it as one of the world's greatest masterpieces of literature. However, it is much more than that. It enables us to understand God's great love and his eternal purposes in a unique, though somewhat disconcerting and surprising way. It provides the long-needed key to effective and victorious living under circumstances of pain and sorrow.

HENRY M. MORRIS

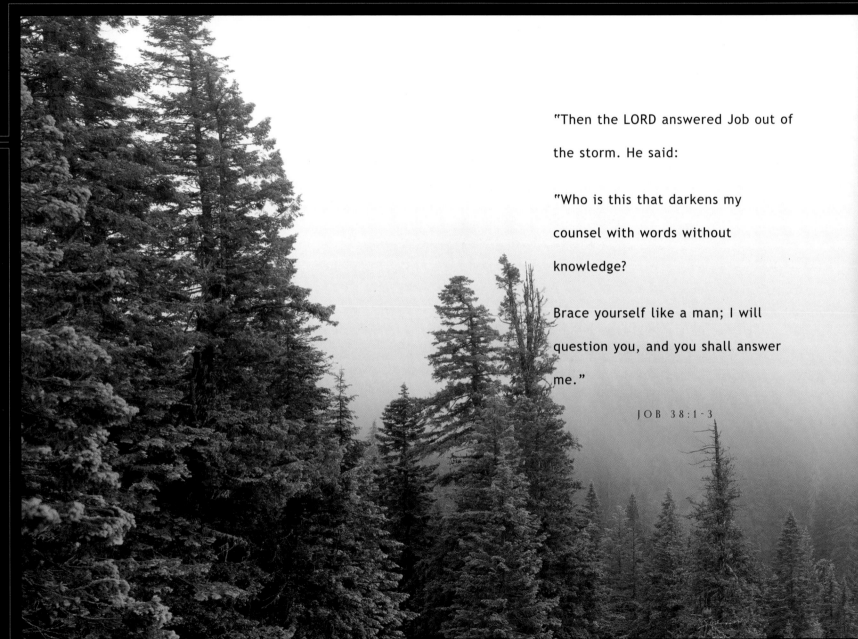

"Then the LORD answered Job out of the storm. He said:

"Who is this that darkens my counsel with words without knowledge?

Brace yourself like a man; I will question you, and you shall answer me."

JOB 38:1-3

"Where were you when I laid the

earth's foundation?

Tell me if you understand.

Who marked off its dimensions?

Surely you know!"

JOB 38:4,5

"Who stretched a measuring line across it?

On what were its footings set, or who laid its cornerstone — while the morning stars sang together and all the angels shouted for joy?"

JOB 38:5-7

I f humans are ever to "subdue the earth" as God commanded, they must understand, first of all, its wonderful origin. Strange and imaginative have been the various cosmogonies invented by ancient pagan evolutionists and modern "scientific" evolutionists. To all such speculations, God rejoins: "How could you possibly know what happened? Were you there?"

HENRY M. MORRIS

"Who shut up the sea behind doors   when I made the clouds its garment

when it burst forth from the womb,   and wrapped it in thick darkness."

"When I fixed limits for it and set

its doors and bars in place, when I

said, 'This far you may come and no

farther; here is where your proud

waves halt'?"

JOB 38:10, 11

The earth is the Lord's, and everything in it, the world, and all who live in it;

for he founded it upon the seas and established it upon the waters.

PSALMS 24:1

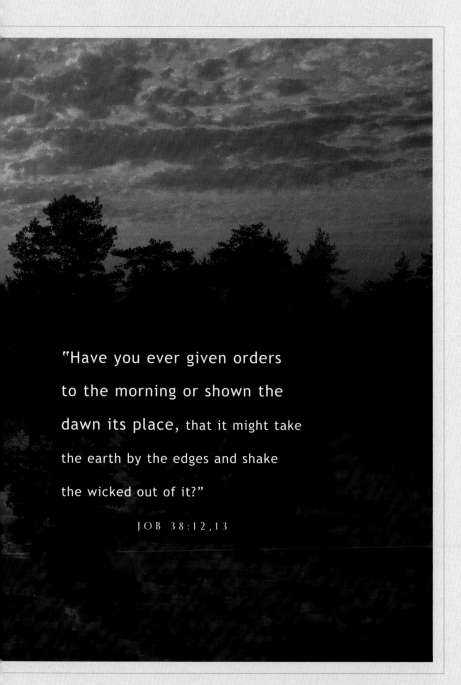

"Have you ever given orders
to the morning or shown the
dawn its place, that it might take
the earth by the edges and shake
the wicked out of it?"

JOB 38:12,13

*The heavens
declare the glory
of God; the skies
proclaim the work
of his hands. Day
after day they pour
forth speech; night
after night they
display knowledge.*

*There is no speech
or language where their voice is not heard. Their voice
goes out into all the earth, their words to the ends of the
world. In the heavens he has pitched a tent for the sun,
which is like a bridegroom coming from his pavilion, like
a champion rejoicing to run his course. It rises at one
end of the heavens and makes its circuit to the other;
nothing is hidden from its heat.*

PSALMS 19:1-6

"The earth takes shape like clay under a seal; its features stand out like those of a garment. The wicked are denied their light, and their upraised arm is broken."

Surely the nations are like a drop in a bucket;

they are regarded as dust on the scales; he weighs

the islands as though they were fine dust.

ISAIAH 40:15

"Have you journeyed to the springs

of the sea or walked in the recesses

of the deep?"

JOB 38:16

"Have the gates of death been shown to you?

Have you seen the gates of the shadow of death?"

JOB 38:17

"Have you comprehended the vast

expanses of the earth?

Tell me, if you know all this."

JOB 38:18

God moves in a mysterious way His wonders to perform;

He plants his footsteps in the sea And rides upon the storm.

WILLIAM COWPER

LIGHT SHINING OUT OF DARKNESS

"What is the way to the abode of light?"

JOB 38:19

God is day and night, winter and summer; war and peace, satiety and want.

HERACLITUS
FRAGMENTS

"And where does darkness reside? Can you take them to their places? Do you know the paths to their dwellings? Surely you know, for you were already born! You have lived so many years!"

JOB 38:19

"Have you entered the storehouses of the snow or seen the storehouses of the hail, which I reserve for times of trouble, for days of war and battle?"

JOB 38:22, 23

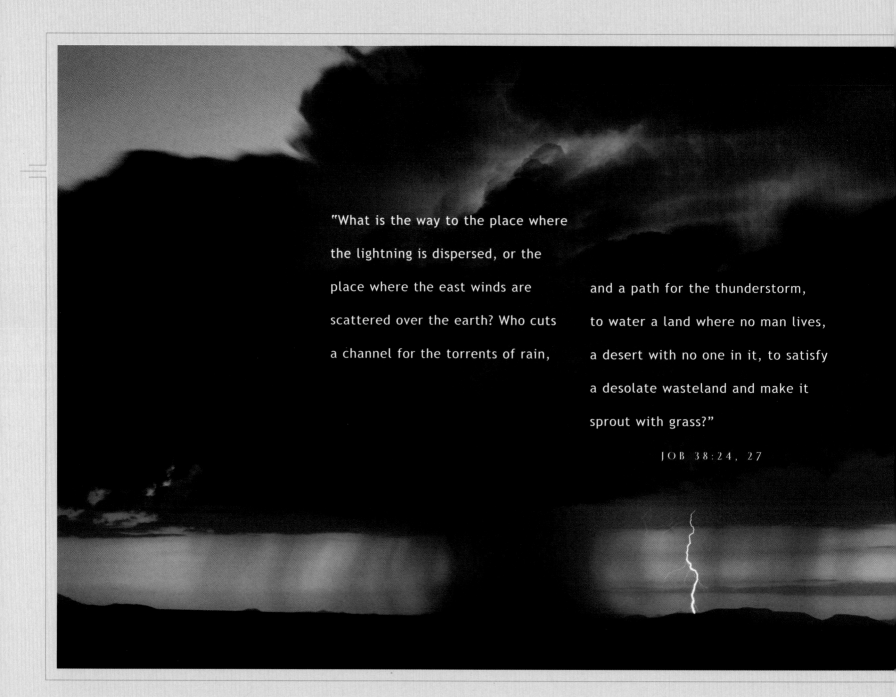

"What is the way to the place where the lightning is dispersed, or the place where the east winds are scattered over the earth? Who cuts a channel for the torrents of rain, and a path for the thunderstorm, to water a land where no man lives, a desert with no one in it, to satisfy a desolate wasteland and make it sprout with grass?"

JOB 38:24, 27

God never wrought miracles to convince atheism,

because his ordinary works convince it.

FRANCIS BACON

"Does the rain have a father?

Who fathers the drops of dew?"

JOB 38:28

God is seen in the star, in the stone, in the flesh, in the soul and the clod.

ROBERT BROWNING
"SAUL," MEN AND WOMEN

T he Bible reveals that hope exists. In fact, even "the invisible things of Him from the creation of the world are clearly seen, being understood by the things that are made, even His eternal power and Godhead, so that they are without excuse" (Romans 1:20). Thus, by studying the creation—the things that are made—we ought to be able to accurately determine certain things, especially the fact that things were made by something or Someone separate from the creation, an entity that was not made in the same fashion as everything else.

JOHN D. MORRIS

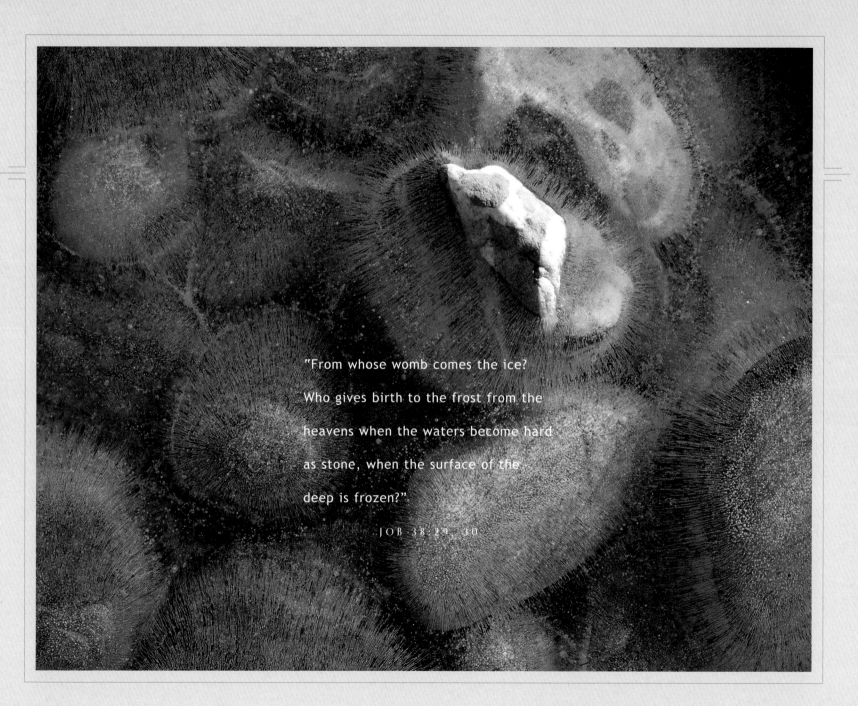

"From whose womb comes the ice?

Who gives birth to the frost from the

heavens when the waters become hard

as stone, when the surface of the

deep is frozen?"

JOB 38:29, 30

The world is charged with the grandeur of God.

GERALD MANLEY HOPKINS
GOD'S GRANDEUR

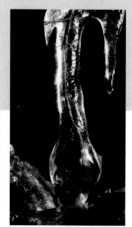

This goodness of God is evidenced in the daily victory of light over darkness, the annual return of spring after winter, and especially the oft-repeated triumph of life over death. Although individuals die, new souls are born, and life goes on, and always there is hope.

HENRY M. MORRIS

"Can you bind the beautiful

Pleiades? Can you loose the cords

of Orion? Can you bring forth the

constellations in their season or lead

out the Bear with its cubs? Do you

know the laws of the heavens? Can

you set up God's dominion over the

earth?"

JOB 38:31-33

My soul, there is a country
Far beyond the stars,
Where stands a winged sentry
All skilful in the wars:
There, above noise and danger,
Sweet Peace is crowned
with smiles,
And One born in a manger
Commands the beauteous files.

HENRY VAUGHAN

I see His blood upon
the rose And in the stars
the glory of His eyes.

JOSEPH MARY
PLUNKETT

From a biblical perspective, Romans 1 teaches that the evidence for creation is all around us and, therefore, anyone who does not believe in the Creator and Saviour is condemned. It is also important to recognize that one does not have to see the Creator to recognize the fact of special creation. Just because one cannot see the architect and builder who designed and constructed a house does not mean that there was not an intelligent designer behind it.

KEN HAM

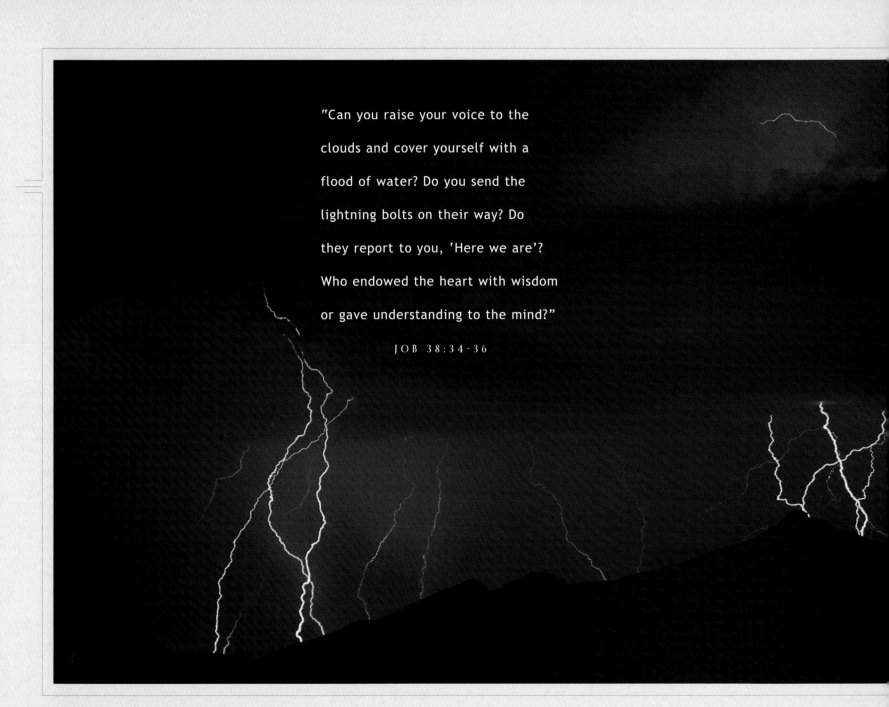

"Can you raise your voice to the
clouds and cover yourself with a
flood of water? Do you send the
lightning bolts on their way? Do
they report to you, 'Here we are'?
Who endowed the heart with wisdom
or gave understanding to the mind?"

JOB 38:34-36

We think the power of a lightning or thunderstorm is immense. But this is nothing compared to the power God exercised in creating the smallest cell.

KEN HAM

In all the many, many [Scripture] references to creation, there is not the slightest hint that any process of "evolution" could ever be regarded as God's method of creation.

HENRY M. MORRIS

"Who has the wisdom to count the clouds?"

JOB 38:37

The power that holds the sky's majesty wins our worship.

AESCHYLUS

"Who can tip over the water jars of

the heavens when the dust becomes

hard and the clods of earth stick

together?"

JOB 38:37, 38

What can be more foolish than to think that all this rare fabric

of heaven and earth could come by chance, when all

the skill of science is not able to make an oyster.

JEREMY TAYLOR

"Do you hunt the prey for the lioness and satisfy the hunger of the lions when they crouch in their dens or lie in wait in a thicket? Who provides food for the raven when its young cry out to God and wander about for lack of food?"

JOB 38:39-41

If every gnat that flies were
an archangel, all that could
but tell me that there is
a God, and the poorest
worm that creeps
tells me that.

JOHN DONNE
SERMONS

"Do you know when the mountain goats give birth? Do you watch when the doe bears her fawn? Do you count the months till they bear? Do you know the time they give birth? They crouch down and bring forth their young; their labor pains are ended. Their young thrive and grow strong in the wilds; they leave and do not return."

JOB 39:1-4

Will the wild ox consent to serve you?
Will he stay by your manger at night?
Can you hold him to the furrow with
a harness? Will he till the valleys
behind you? Will you rely on him for
his great strength? Will you leave
your heavy work to him? Can you
trust him to bring in your grain and
gather it to your threshing floor?"

JOB 39:5-12

"Who let the wild donkey go free? Who untied his ropes? I gave him the wasteland as his home, the salt flats as his habitat. He laughs at the commotion in the town; he does not hear a driver's shout. He ranges the hills for his pasture and searches for any green thing.

The Creator of the earth is the owner of it.

JOHN WOOLMAN

"The wings of the ostrich flap joyfully, but they cannot compare with the pinions and feathers of the stork. She lays her eggs on the ground and lets them warm in the

her with wisdom or give her a share of good sense. Yet

sand, unmindful that a foot may crush them, that some wild animal may trample them. She treats her young harshly, as if they were not hers; she cares not that her labor was in vain, for God did not endow

when she spreads her feathers to run, she laughs at horse and rider."

JOB 39:13-18

Earth, with her thousand voices, praises God.

SAMUEL TAYLOR COLERIDGE

"HYMN BEFORE SUNRISE"

"Do you give the horse his strength or clothe his neck with a flowing mane? Do you make him leap like a locust, striking terror with his proud snorting? He paws fiercely, rejoicing in his strength, and charges into the fray. He laughs at fear, afraid of nothing; he does not shy away from the sword. The quiver rattles against his side, along with the flashing spear and lance. In frenzied excitement he eats up the ground; he cannot stand still when the trumpet sounds. At the blast of the trumpet he snorts, 'Aha!' He catches the scent of battle from afar, the shout of commanders and the battle cry."

JOB 39:19-25

God is the perfect poet, Who in his person acts his own creations.

ROBERT BROWNING
PARACELSUS

How great is our Creator God! How far above our ways and understandings are His! Did you know that the number of possible combinations of genes within each kind of creature is more than the number of the stars in the universe? What creativity! What marvelous design! What a small glimpse of His infinite power, wisdom, and knowledge!

KEN HAM

"Does the hawk take flight by your wisdom and spread his wings toward the south?

Does the eagle soar at your command and build his nest on high? He dwells on a cliff and stays there at night; a rocky crag is his stronghold. From there he seeks out his food; his eyes detect it from afar. His young ones feast on blood, and where the slain are, there he is."

JOB 39:26-30

If you get simple beauty and nought else, You get about the best thing God invents.

ROBERT BROWNING
FRA LIPPO LIPPI

The LORD said to Job:

"Will the one who contends with the Almighty correct him? Let him who accuses God answer him!"

Then Job answered the LORD:

"I am unworthy — how can I reply to you? I put my hand over my mouth. I spoke once, but I have no answer, twice but I will say no more."

JOB 40:1-5

Instead of complaining that God had hidden

Himself, you will give Him thanks for

having revealed so much of Himself.

PASCAL, PENSÉES

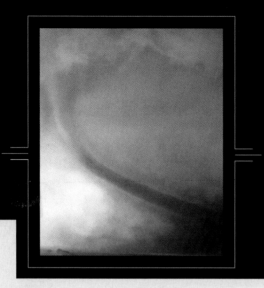

Then the LORD spoke to Job out of the storm:

"Brace yourself like a man; I will question you, and you shall answer me.

Would you discredit my justice? Would you condemn me to justify yourself? Do you have an arm like God's, and can your voice thunder like his? Then adorn yourself with glory and splendor, and clothe yourself in honor and majesty.

Unleash the fury of your wrath, look at every proud man and bring him low, look at every proud man and humble him, crush the wicked where they stand. Bury them all in the dust together; shroud their faces in the grave. Then I myself will admit to you that your own right hand can save you."

JOB 40:6-14

*If I stoop into a dark
tremendous sea of cloud,
It is but for a time;
I press God's lamp
Close to my breast;
its splendour, soon or late,
Will pierce the gloom:
I shall emerge one day.*

ROBERT BROWNING

N ot long after the flood, a man called Job heard God describe a great creature that Job was obviously familiar with. God was showing Job how great He was as Creator, in causing him to observe the largest land animal He had made: "Behold now behemoth, which I made with thee . . ."

KEN HAM

"Look at the behemoth, which I made along with you and which feeds on grass like an ox. What strength he has in his loins, what power in the muscles of his belly! His tail sways like a cedar; the sinews of his thighs are close-knit. His

bones are tubes of bronze, his limbs like rods of iron. He ranks first among the works of God, yet his Maker can approach him with his sword. The hills bring him their produce, and all the wild animals play nearby. Under the lotus plants he lies, hidden among the reeds

in the marsh. The lotuses conceal him in their shadow; the poplars by the stream surround him. When the river rages, he is not alarmed; he is secure, though the Jordan should surge against his mouth. Can anyone capture him by the eyes, or trap him and pierce his nose?"

JOB 40:15-24

Nature is the art of God.

DANTE

ON WORLD GOVERNMENT (C. 1313)

God designed each animal with equipment and behavior needed for its survival. The equipment for protecting, or built-in defenses, includes special colors or shapes, weapons, and protective coverings. Every plant and animal is perfectly designed for its environment.

KEN HAM

"Can you pull in the leviathan with a fishhook or tie down his tongue with a rope? Can you put a cord through his nose or pierce his jaw with a hook? Will he keep begging you for mercy? Will he speak to you with gentle words? Will he make an agreement with you for you to take him as your slave for life? Can you make a pet of him like a bird or put him on a leash for your girls? Will traders barter for him? Will they divide him up among the merchants? Can you fill his hide with harpoons or his head with fishing spears? If you lay a hand on him, you will remember the struggle and never do it again! Any hope of subduing him is false; the mere sight of him is overpowering. No one is fierce enough to rouse him. Who then is able to stand against me? Who has a claim against me that I must pay? Everything under heaven belongs to me."

JOB 41:1-11

T he best that modern expositors have been able to do is to call behemoth an elephant and leviathan a crocodile. But such definitions are impossible. For example, behemoth "moveth his tail like a cedar" and leviathan is a fearsome monster whose "breath kindleth coals, and a flame goeth out of his mouth" (Job 40:17; 41:21). Whatever these extinct animals may have been, they were not elephants and crocodiles! The most likely conclusion is that they were what modern paleontologists have called dinosaurs (and what ancient historians called dragons) . . . They were real animals, not mythical animals, and some at least were still living in Job's day . . .

HENRY M. MORRIS

All things bright and beautiful,

All creatures great and

small, All things wise

and wonderful — The

Lord God made them all.

CECIL FRANCES ALEXANDER

"I will not fail to speak of his limbs, his strength and his graceful form. Who can strip off his outer coat? Who would approach him with a bridle? Who dares open the doors of his mouth, ringed about with his fearsome teeth? His back has rows of shields tightly sealed together; each is so close to the next that no air can pass between. They are joined fast to one another; they cling together and cannot be parted.

His snorting throws out flashes of light; his eyes are like the rays of dawn. Firebrands stream from his mouth; sparks of fire shoot out. Smoke pours from his nostrils as a boiling pot over a fire of reeds. His breath sets coals ablaze, and flames dart from his mouth. Strength resides in his neck; dismay goes before him. The folds of his flesh are tightly joined; they are firm and immovable. His chest is

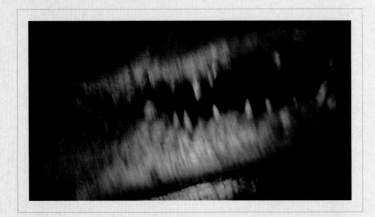

Others went out on the sea in ships; they were merchants on the mighty waters. They saw the works of the Lord, his wonderful deeds in the deep.

PSALMS 107:23-24

hard as rock, hard as a lower millstone. When he rises up, the mighty are terrified; they retreat before his thrashing. The sword that reaches him has no effect, nor does the spear or the dart or the javelin. Iron he treats like straw and bronze like rotten wood. Arrows do not make him flee; slingstones are like chaff to him. A club seems to him but a piece of straw; he laughs at the rattling of the lance. His undersides are jagged potsherds, leaving a trail in the mud like a threshing sledge."

JOB 41:12-30

I long for scenes where man hath never

trod. A place where woman never smiled

or wept — There to abide with my Creator,

God, And Sleep as I in childhood sweetly slept,

Untroubling, and untroubled where I lie,

The grass below — above the vaulted sky.

JOHN CLARE

"I Am"

Even what man considers
to be one of the lowliest of
animals, is, in fact, an exquisite
and marvelous testimony to the
handiwork of our Creator God
— invoking a deep sense of
awe, wonder, and praise.

KEN HAM

The heavens call to you, and circle around you, displaying to you

their eternal splendours, and your eye gazes only to earth.

DANTE

"PURGATORIO," THE DIVINE COMEDY

All are but parts of one stupendous whole,

Whose body Nature is, and God the soul.

ALEXANDER POPE

AN ESSAY ON MAN

"He makes the depths churn like a boiling caldron and stirs up the sea like a pot of ointment. Behind him he leaves a glistening wake; one would think the deep had white hair. Nothing on earth is his equal — a creature without fear. He looks down on all that are haughty; he is king over all that are proud."

Then Job replied to the LORD:

"I know that you can do all things;

no plan of yours can be thwarted.

You asked, 'Who is this that obscures

my counsel without knowledge?'

Surely I spoke of things I did not

understand, things too wonderful for

me to know.

"You said, 'Listen now, and I will

speak; I will question you, and you

shall answer me.'"

JOB 42:1-4

"My ears had heard of you but

now my eyes have seen you."

JOB 42:5

I n the physical realm, light is manifested especially in the glory of visible light, but actually includes the entire electromagnetic spectrum of forces and energies, pervading the entire universe. The source of all such physical power is God, "dwelling in the light which no man can approach unto" (1 Timothy 6:16).

HENRY M. MORRIS

The Bible teaches unequivocally that the Creator is a great person who created the entire universe of space and time, as well as matter and energy and all the systems and personalities that exist in the space/time universe. The creator is neither the "Mother Earth" of the ancient pagan pantheists nor the 'cosmic consciousness' of modern pantheists, and certainly not the light of "evolution" as promoted by New-Age philosophers. The Creator is God, Elohim, the uni-plural God set forth in the most profound and probably most ancient words ever written: "In the beginning God created the heaven and the earth' (Gen. 1:1)."

HENRY M. MORRIS

I think that I shall never see,

a poem lovely as a tree.

Poems are made by fools like me,

but only God can make a tree.

{ALFRED} JOYCE KILMER

A FRENCH POET

O God within my breast,

Almighty! Ever-present Deity!

Life — that in me has rest,

As Io'undying Life — have power in Thee!

Vain are the thousand creeds

That move men's hearts: unutterably vain;

Worthless as withered weeds,

Or idlest froth amid the boundless main.

So surely anchor'd on

The steadfast rock of immortality.

EMILY BRONTE

E arth's crammed with heaven,

And every common bush afire

with God;

But only he who sees, takes off his shoes,

The rest sit round it and pluck blackberries,

And daub their natural faces unaware

More and more from the first similitude.

ELIZABETH
BARRETT
BROWNING

I t is important that we examine closely

God's monologue on creation and

providence in Job 38-41. These are the

truths God wanted Job and his counselors

to know in ancient times, and we will find

that they are even more relevant for our

own times.

HENRY M. MORRIS

N o coward soul is mine,

No trembler in the world's

storm-troubled sphere:

I see Heaven's glories shine,

And faith shines equal, arming me

from fear.

EMILY BRONTE